Qadira,

You are beautiful
inside *and* out!

♡ always,
Mey [illegible]

Written by Ndija Anderson-Yantha
Illustrated by Kaela Beals

Edited by Marlo Garnsworthy
Graphic edits by Dylan Gnitecki

Thank you to everyone who believed in and
supported this vision, from conception to completion.

For still the vision awaits its appointed time; it hastens to the end—it will not lie. If it seems slow, wait for it; it will surely come; it will not delay.

–Habakkuk 2:3 ESV

To every girl who has been told that her hair isn't "good" enough: you are beautiful just the way you are!

ISBN: 978-0-9958577-0-4

Creative Directors: Ndija Anderson-Yantha and Matthew Yantha

Illustrator: Kaela Beals; Editor: Marlo Garnsworthy; Graphic Editor: Dylan Gnitecki

www.thenaturalhairadvocate.com

My name is Zuri, but everyone knows
me as "the girl with the puffy hair."
My hair is super-big, curly, and fuzzy.

It grows out, and even gravity
can't hold it down!

Sometimes my hair likes to do its own thing, and it gets all tangly, so when my mother used to comb it, I'd scream,

"Pleeeease, just cut it off!"

because it would hurt so much.

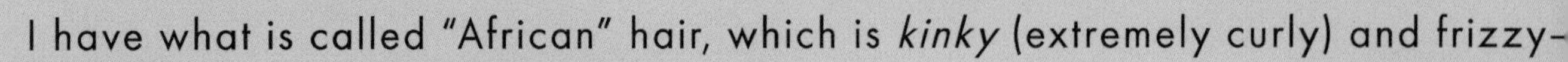
I have what is called "African" hair, which is *kinky* (extremely curly) and frizzy–

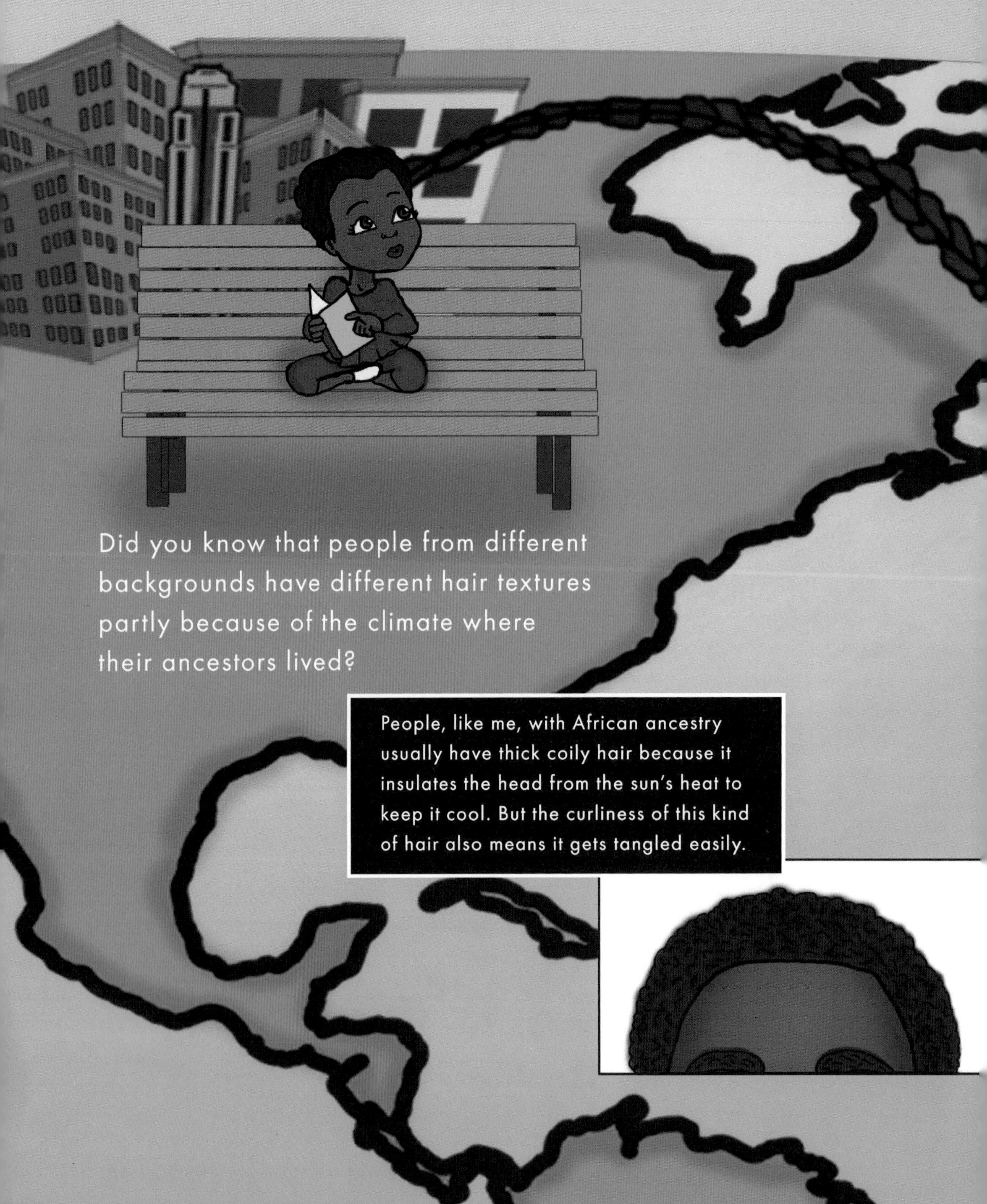

Did you know that people from different backgrounds have different hair textures partly because of the climate where their ancestors lived?

People, like me, with African ancestry usually have thick coily hair because it insulates the head from the sun's heat to keep it cool. But the curliness of this kind of hair also means it gets tangled easily.

the same type of hair as my ancestors who came from *Sub-Saharan Africa.*

Sometimes the kids at school—and sometimes even my cousins—ask me, "What are you gonna do with that hair? Why don't you just *perm* it?"

"Why should I?" I say.
"I think my hair is wonderful, and
I wouldn't have it any other way!"

Now that I know how to take care of my hair myself, I don't want to straighten it.

The unique texture of my hair means I can shape it and design it any way I want. I can turn it into beautiful works of African art and be proud of my heritage.

And if your hair is curly like mine, then that means you can do it, too. I'll show you!

You can braid it!

Braids are made by intertwining three or more strands of hair together.

You can crisscross your hair into thick plaits,

into teeny-tiny single braids, or any size in-between.

Are you aware that hair braiding is an ancient African art?

The ancient Egyptians were probably the first people to wear their hair in braided styles. Archaeologists have found artwork in ancient Egyptian tombs showing all kinds of hairdos—wigs, extensions, braids, and twists—that were worn by people from all walks of life, thousands of years ago.

Even royals, like *Queen Nefertari* (the wife of Ramses II, 13th century BC), wore their hair in braids back then!

Frescoes in her tomb show the queen wearing thin single braids held together with gold thread at the ends, to keep them from coming undone.

Since the time of the Ancient Egyptians, braids have been worn in different forms by humans all around the world, and they are still very popular today in many places, such as India.

But nowhere did braiding take off like it did in Africa!

In Africa, hairstyling—and hair braiding, especially—was an art form, like sculpting.

Braiding soon became a favourite social and cultural pastime all over the African continent because it gave people lots of time to chit-chat during the many hours it took to create the hairdos.

As the strands of hair were being drawn tightly together to create beautiful styles, so too were the relationships between the braider and the hairstyle wearer.

Hair braiding also gave the artistic members of a community a chance to show off their creative skills!

African hairdos were very fancy, often combining different styling methods, such as braiding, wrapping, cutting, and shaved patterns all into one hairstyle!

Beads, flowers, coins, shells, and strips of cloth were hair accessories of choice and were braided into the 'dos.

Each hairstyle had a meaning and could tell you important information about the wearer, such as:

age,

gender,

religious beliefs,

social status,

where he or she was from,

and sometimes even a person's family name.

Did you know that braiding connects Black people back to Africa?

EUROP

NORTH AMERICA

WEST INDIES

Braiding is one of the few African practices that survived the *Middle Passage.*

AFRICA

SOUTH AMERICA

Human cargo on a slave ship

THE MIDDLE PASSAGE

The *Middle Passage*, or the crossing of the Atlantic Ocean, was the middle portion of the slaves' trip from Africa to the *New World* during the *Transatlantic Slave Trade*.

House slaves, both male and female, wore their hair in braids and *cornrows* to keep it tidy and presentable for their slave masters.

Field slaves plaited, cornrowed, and *threaded* (tightly wrapped with cloth or thread) their hair to keep it out of their faces as they worked in the fields. Field slaves also used *bandannas* (or "head ties") to shield their heads from bugs, the sun's heat, and the shame of not being able to take care of their hair like they used to in Africa.

Many Black women still use head ties to protect their tresses when they go to sleep or to cover their heads when their hair is not done.

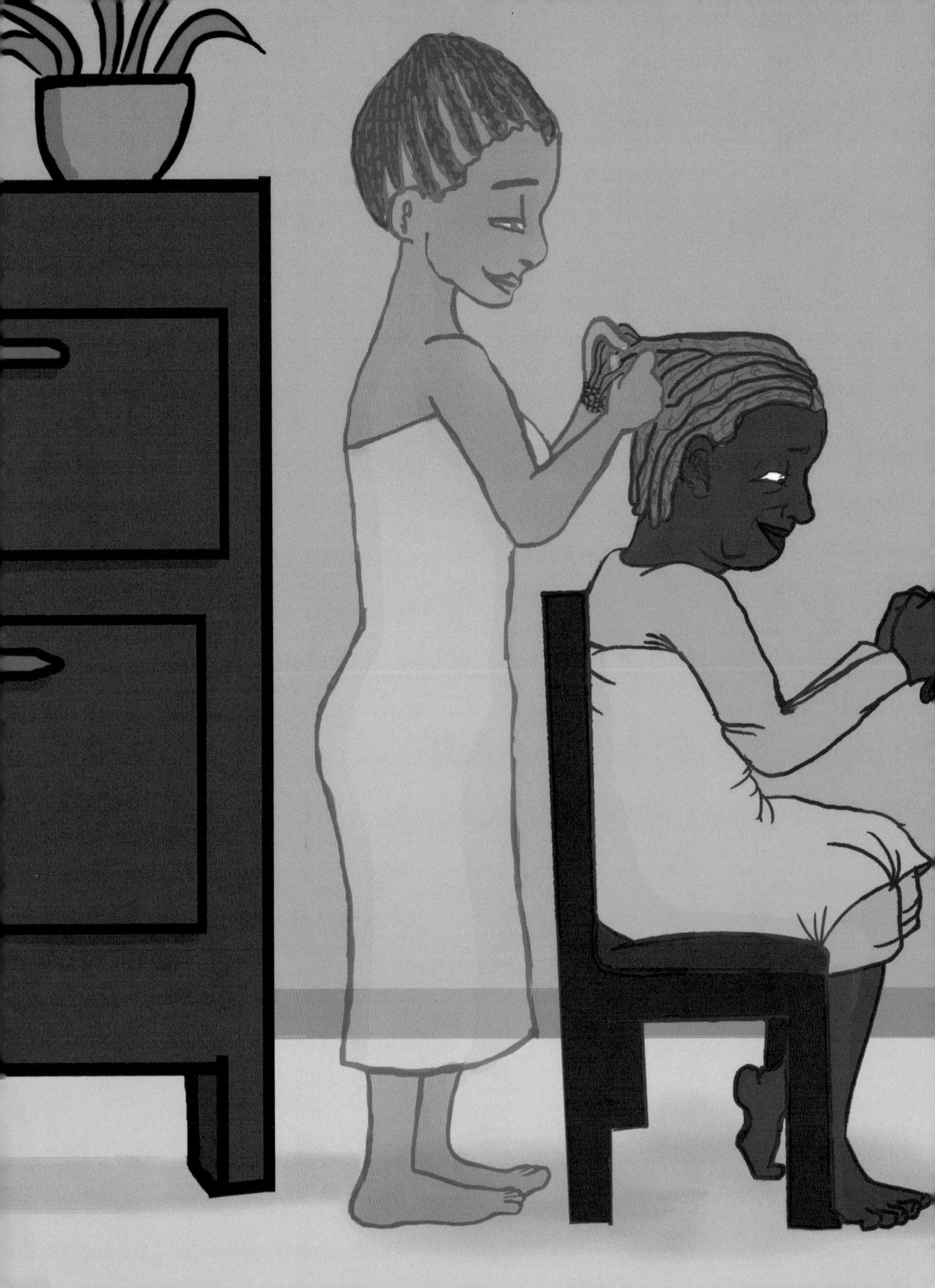

Slave women would teach their daughters how to braid, and so the tradition was passed from the hands of grandmothers to mothers to daughters, tying their hairstyles to their African roots.

You can cornrow it!

Cornrows or *canerows* (or track braids) are a traditional African braiding technique.

Cornrows are made by braiding the hair onto the scalp's surface, after parting the hair into a design.

This hairdo was also seen as a symbol for civilization, agriculture, and order.

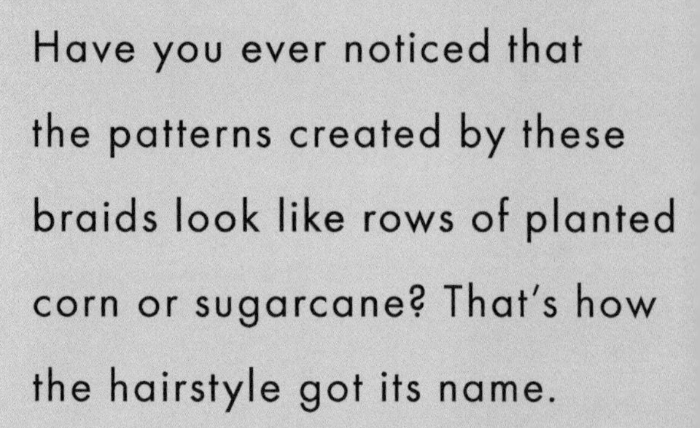

Have you ever noticed that the patterns created by these braids look like rows of planted corn or sugarcane? That's how the hairstyle got its name.

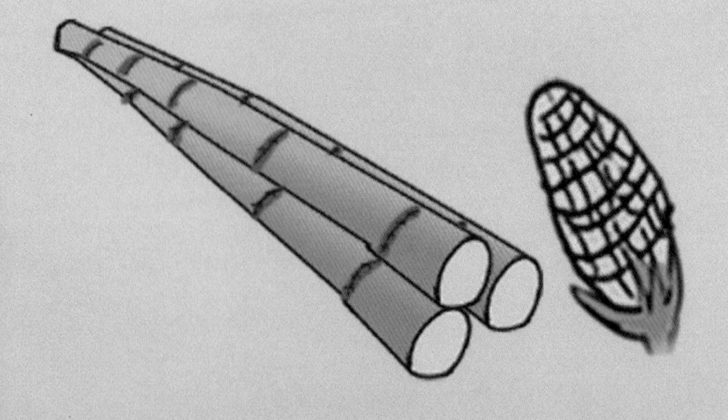

In Africa, cornrow styles had specific meanings—certain styles were created for religious ceremonies, war, festivals, or *rites of passage*.

Unfortunately, many of the special meanings were lost during slavery.

Although slaves in the New World wore cornrows to keep their hair neat and tidy, only children would wear them in public because African hairstyles were considered inappropriate,

so, for hundreds of years, people thought braids were only for kids.

However, in the 1960s and 1970s, when Blacks began to get back in touch with their African roots during the *Black Power Movement*, cornrows became an acceptable and a much-loved hairdo for adults again.

It wasn't until the 1990s (thanks to rap and hip-hop artists) that cornrows were embraced worldwide—

and in the 2000s, even celebrities and international runway models can be seen wearing them!

You can twist it!

Twists are similar to braids, except they are made by intertwining two strands of hair instead of three.

Twists have been a long-time style of choice in many African groups, such as the *Afars* (or *Danakils*) and the *Karrayyus* in the *horn of Africa* and peoples from the *Maghreb region* (North Africa).

Did you realize that there are several different ways to twist your hair?

Two-strand twists are the basic form of the style and are usually made using your own hair. There are other forms of twists that are made by using different textures of *extension hair.*

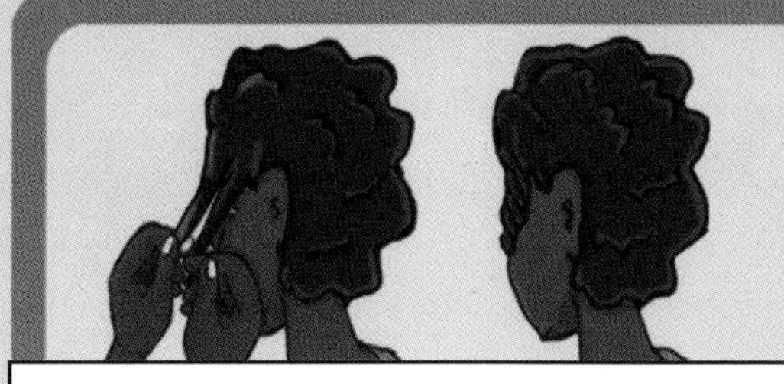

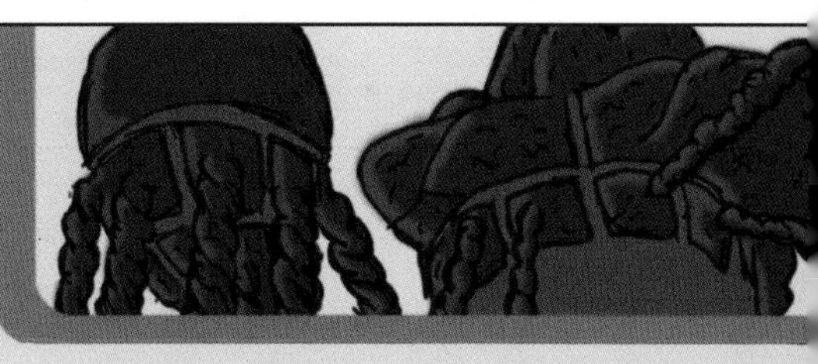

Senegalese twists or *rope twists*, which look like tiny ropes, are long twists made with sleek extension hair.

Have you heard the term "Senegalese" before? "Senegalese" refers to someone or something from Senegal, a West African country that borders Mauritania, Mali, Guinea, Guinea-Bissau, and the Gambia. Senegalese women have been known for being master braiders.

Kinky twists are short, two-strand twists made using kinky extension hair.

Marley twists are long, like Senegalese twists, but are made by using frizzier extension hair.

Havana twists are chunky versions of kinky twists.

You can flat-twist it!

Flat-twists are similar to cornrows, only you create them with two strands of hair rather than three.

Or you can untwist these styles into what's called a *twist-out*.

Bantu and Zulu people are found in Sub-Saharan Africa, while Nubians come from southern Egypt and northern Sudan.

You can bantu-knot it!

Bantu knots, which are also known as *Zulu* or *Nubian knots*, *chiney bumps*, *pepper seeds*, or *hair nubbins,* are made by sectioning your hair into triangles, diamonds, or squares and coiling those sections into knots.

This knotted hairstyle has been worn for centuries by girls throughout the African continent and the Caribbean. *Bantu*, *Zulu,* and *Nubian* are all names of ethnic groups in Africa.

In some Caribbean countries, this hairstyle is called *pepper seeds* because of how the knots look.

In the past, Bantu knots were usually only worn around the house—

especially after washing and detangling your hair because the knots help to stretch your curls out—

but nowadays both girls and women can be seen wearing their knots everywhere.

You can also give yourself a *Bantu knot-out!*

You can thread it!

Threading (or wrapping) is another ancient African styling method.

To thread your hair, you tightly wrap sections of your hair with thread or cloth.

You've probably seen this technique before and did not even realize it: amusement parks or fairs often have booths where you can get your hair wrapped with brightly coloured thread.

People also get hair wrapped when they travel to tropical vacation spots, such as Brazil, where they are called *tererês*.

In the 1800s, slave women would use threading to help them create the straight White hairstyles of the day by stretching the curls out of their kinky hair.

The slave women would tie their hair down in a *bandanna* (or "head-tie") during the week to keep the threaded sections from unravelling...

It was also easier to keep threaded hair off their faces as they worked in the fields, and they would keep their hairstyles hidden under their bandannas.

...before it was time to reveal their straightened hairdos at church the next Sunday or for other special occasions.

After church service and other events, the women would re-thread their hair and tie it down again for the upcoming week.

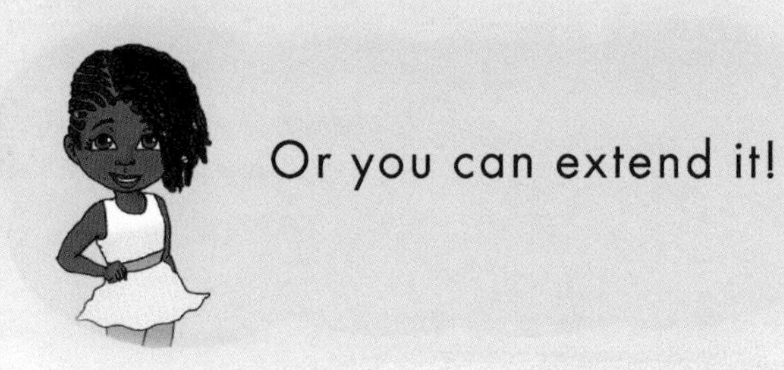

Hair extensions are extra pieces of *synthetic* (man-made) or human hair that are added to give length or body to a braided style.

Extensions come in a variety of shades and colours, lengths, and textures.

People have been wearing false hair since around 3000 BC, starting with the ancient Egyptians, who were among the first humans to wear extensions.

When the mummy of *Queen Meryet-Amen* (daughter of Ramses II and Queen Nefertari) was discovered, she still had several braid extensions attached to her head. Some of her other single braids were found curled up together in a basket in her tomb!

Fake hair was very trendy in ancient Egypt—almost everyone wore wigs made of black wool, cotton, human hair, palm-leaf fibers, or horsehair—and the Egyptians who could not afford wigs would create similar looks using hair extensions.

You can naturally crimp it!

Undoing any of these hairstyles—whether braided, cornrowed, twisted, or threaded—will give you crimps without the need to apply heat to your hair.

You could even lock it!

"Dreadlocks" or *"dreads"* is a rope-like hairstyle created by coiling your hair into sections and allowing it to grow without combing it.

"Dread-locks" have really been given a bad name.

Some believe that the first part of the name, "dread", came from slavery, when White people would call the tangled, matted hair of the slaves "dreadful."

Rastafarians believe that the term comes from the fear of the "*dread-ful* power of the holy," in other words, the awesome power of God.

Regardless of where the name came from, many wearers of this hairdo have dropped the "a" from the word "dread" to remove any negative meanings.

Curlier hair locks faster than straighter hair, which is why African hair is the easiest to dredlock.

The "locks" part of the name comes from how the hairstyle is formed: when hair is left uncombed, it naturally clumps together and forms into "locks."

When people see someone with 'locks, they often think of Bob Marley and *Rastafarianism*, or they make negative assumptions about a dred-locked person's hygiene, politics, or social class, based on stereotypes.

Both Samson and John the Baptist in the Bible had 'locks. As *Nazirites* (holy men in ancient Judaism), they took a vow to never cut their hair, so they allowed it to grow naturally, without interference.

But would you believe that 'locks have actually been a hairstyle of honour for thousands of years?

Hindu *sadhus* (holy men) and Ethiopian Coptic priests have also worn dredlocks as a sign of their holiness.

And even ancient Egyptian kings are believed to have worn them as their crowning glory!

Like the Nazirites, Rastafarians believe that the Bible requires holy people to not change the state of their hair. When someone joins the Rastafarian faith, they leave their hair to grow, and it eventually begins to lock.

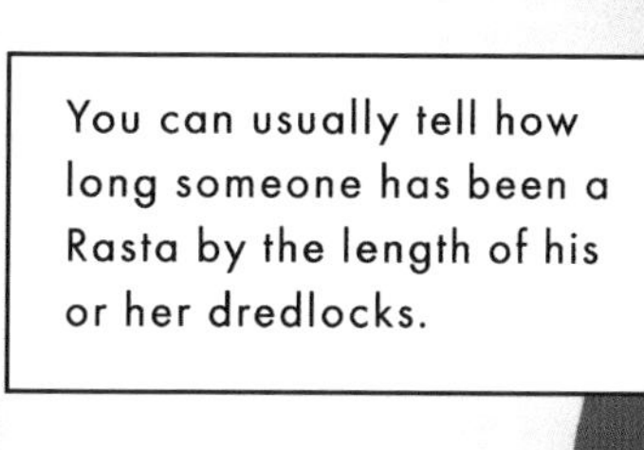

Rastas were also inspired to wear 'locks by two different dredlocked groups in Kenya: the *Kikuyu* (or *Mau Mau*) soldiers who rebelled against the British in the 1950s, and *Masai* warriors, who wear 'locks that are dyed red using plant extracts.

Hamer women in Ethiopia and *Himba* women in Namibia also wear their hair in dredlocked hairstyles.

Although Rastafarians wear their hair in 'locks for religious reasons and to celebrate their Black pride, 'locks are a hairstyle that has been enjoyed by people of various ethnic backgrounds, hair textures, and belief systems, such as: the ancient Greeks, Romans, and *Germanic tribes*; the *Aztecs*; the *Naga Indians*; North American *indigenous* peoples; and *Pacific Islanders.*

White people wear dredlocks, too: in Australia, for example, dredlocks have become popular with surfers, as well as curly-haired Aussies, who prefer to 'lock their hair rather than struggle with their tangles.

You could let it go
and just 'fro it!

An *Afro* or a *'fro* is a hairstyle formed by patting curly hair into a round shape.

This African hairdo, which used to be known as the "bush" or the "natural," became a trend for South African women in the 1950s.

(This hairstyle is the equivalent of wearing African hair "down," so it had also been worn by other peoples, such as the *Karrayyu* people of Ethiopia.)

During the 1960s, the "bush" was re-discovered by Blacks in the United States, when it became known as the "Afro." The Afro was the symbol of the Black Power Movement by making the bold statement that "Black is Beautiful!"

When African-Americans began wearing their Afros with pride, Native Americans were encouraged to celebrate their heritage, too, and they began embracing their traditional clothing and braided hairstyles in their own Red Power Movement!

Or fro-hawk it!

A *fro-hawk* is a mix between an Afro and a *Mohawk*.

A *Mohawk* or a *Mohican* (or an *Iro*, for "Iroquois") is a Native American hairstyle made by shaving the sides of your hair and leaving a ridge of hair down the middle of your head.

To give yourself a fro-hawk, you can either shave the sides of your hair (like a real Mohawk), or simply smooth or braid the sides of your hair upwards while leaving the ends out down the middle of your head.

Although the name "Mohawk" comes from the *Mohawk Nation* (an *indigenous* group, originally from New York State), it has been worn by several different *aboriginal* groups throughout history.

Or Afro-puff it!

Afro-puffs are ponytails made with afro hair.

As you can see, there are so many things that your kinky, coily hair can do, and these basic hairstyles are only a start.

The more I experiment with my hair, the more designs I discover.

Now, when I go to school, everyone asks me,

"*How* did you do that to your hair?"

And my cousins ask me, "*When* can you do that to ours?"

Natural hair is so versatile: it can be worn curly or straight; it can be worn in a beautiful braided style; or just out—and that's what makes it so awesome!

So the next time someone asks you

"What are you gonna do with that hair?",

you can proudly

say to them,

"Anything I want!"

Glossary

Aboriginal: Native people or native culture.

Afars: An ethnic group, who live in the Afar region of Ethiopia, northern Djibouti, and southern Eritrea. Also known as the **Danakils**.

Afro-Latin: Someone or something with both Sub-Saharan African and Latin American origins or roots.

Aztecs: A native people, originally from northern Mexico, whose civilization began in the 13th century in central Mexico and lasted until 1521, during the Spanish conquest.

Bandanna: A square piece of cloth that is tied over the hair, also known as a "head-tie."

Black Power Movement: A political movement from the mid-1960s to the late 1970s, which focused on Black pride and empowerment and fought for equality for people of African descent.

Cornrows or Canerows: A hairstyle of African origin made by parting the hair into sections and braiding it tightly against the scalp.

Dreadlocks or Dredlocks: Rope-like hairstyle created by coiling or twisting the hair into sections (or simply allowing the hair to grow naturally on its own) and leaving the sections to grow without combing them.

Extensions or Extension hair: Extra pieces of human or synthetic (man-made) hair that are added to give length or body to a braided style.

Field Slaves: Slaves who worked out in the fields of the plantation and who typically had darker skin and coily hair.

Frescoes: Paintings done on plaster.

Germanic tribes: Ancient European clans who are believed to have first appeared in modern-day southern Sweden, Denmark, and northern Germany during the Bronze Age (3000 BC-1900 BC). Over thousands of years, these clans spread toward the south and west of Europe and were responsible for ending the Roman Empire in 476 AD.

Hamer: An ethnic group living in southwestern Ethiopia.

Himba: A native group from northern Namibia and southern Angola, whose women are known by the mixture of butter, fat, and red ochre they put on their hair and skin daily.

[The] Horn of Africa: The eastern part of the African continent, including the countries of Ethiopia, Somalia, Eritrea, and Djibouti.

House Slaves: Slaves who worked inside the home, usually with lighter skin and straight or wavy hair, most often the children of White slave owners and Black slave women.

Indigenous: Native people or native culture.

Karrayyu: An ethnic group that lives in the Oromia region of Ethiopia.

Kikuyu or Mau Mau Rebellion: The **Kikuyu** are the largest ethnic group in Kenya. Kikuyu soldiers launched a rebellion, under the name of **Mau Mau**, against British colonial rule from 1952-1960.

Kinky: A term for hair texture that is extremely curly.

[The] Maghreb Region: The northern part of the African continent, including the countries of Morocco, Algeria, Tunisia, and Libya.

Masai or Maasai: An ethnic group living in southern Kenya and northern Tanzania, known for their warriors.

[The] Middle Passage: The middle portion of the slaves' trip from Africa to the New World during the Slave Trade, when the ships crossed the Atlantic Ocean.

Naga Indians: A group of clans who live along the border of India and Myanmar.

Nazirites: In the Hebrew Bible, a Nazirite or Nazarite, refers to a person who voluntarily vowed to be set apart and dedicated to God, as found in Numbers 6:1–21.

[The] New World: The Western Hemisphere, specifically the Americas (including the Caribbean islands and Bermuda).

Pacific Islanders: People from the island groups of the Pacific Ocean, including Polynesia (New Zealand, Fiji, Samoa, Hawaii, Tahiti, Tonga, Easter Island), Melanesia (New Guinea, the Solomon Islands, Vanuatu, New Caledonia), and Micronesia (the Marshall Islands, Palau).

Perm (or Relaxer): A chemical treatment used to straighten kinky or coily hair.

Queen Nefertari: Nefertari (also known as **Nefertari Meritmut**) was one of the Great Royal Wives of Ramses the Great. Nefertari means "beautiful companion" and Meritmut means "Beloved of [the Goddess] Mut." She is one of the best-known Egyptian queens, next to Cleopatra, Nefertiti, and Hatshepsut.

Rastafarianism: A religious and cultural movement that started in Jamaica in the 1950s, whose followers (referred to as **Rastafarians**) believe in the deity of Ethiopian Emperor Haile Selassie I and in the return of his followers to Africa.

Rite of Passage: An event or ritual recognizing an important transition in a person's life, such as puberty or marriage.

Sadhus: Hindu monks.

Sub-Saharan Africa: The African countries that are fully or partially located south of the Sahara Desert, excluding Sudan.

Threading: A styling technique which involves wrapping pieces of hair tightly with thread or cloth.

[The] Transatlantic Slave Trade: The capturing and shipping of West African people by Europeans to the New World, including modern-day Canada, the United States, South America, Central America, and the Caribbean, from the mid-1400s until the 1860s. The middle portion of the slaves' trip, the journey across the Atlantic Ocean, was known as the Middle Passage.

[Two-Strand] Twists: A hairstyle, similar to braids, made by intertwining two hair strands instead of three.

Now it's your turn! To learn how to do the styles in this book (and others), visit:

www.thenaturalhairadvocate.com

66827080R00033

Made in the USA
Charleston, SC
01 February 2017